Enthemonia
(Greek pronunciation
of Eudaimonia)
Contentment & fulfillment

TEN BASIC PRINCIPLES

Ten Basic Principles
That Inspire the Work of Temenos

JOHN CAREY

THE TEMENOS ACADEMY
PATRON HRH THE PRINCE OF WALES

TEMENOS ACADEMY PAPERS NO. 39

First published 2015 by
The Temenos Academy
16 Lincoln's Inn Fields
London WC2A 3ED

www.temenosacademy.org

Registered Charity no. 1043015

ISBN 978 0 9926046 5 3

Typeset and designed by Agnesi Text, Hadleigh
Printed in the United Kingdom
at Smith Settle, Yeadon

Front cover motif © The Estate of Cecil Collins.
The image on the back cover is by Z'ev ben Shimon Halevi;
reproduced with permission.

The Temenos Academy is grateful to Kari Jonassen Tiedemann
for her generosity in sponsoring the publication of this book.

for Stella

. . . Cosi fec' io, poi che me provvide
La Donna mia del suo risponder chiaro,
E come stella in cielo il ver se vide.

PARADISO XXVIII.85–7

CONTENTS

TEN BASIC PRINCIPLES
THAT INSPIRE THE WORK OF TEMENOS

Acknowledgement of Divinity

Love of wisdom, as the essential basis of civilization

Spiritual vision, as the life-breath of civilization

Maintenance of the revered traditions of mankind

Understanding of tradition as continual renewal

The provision of teaching by the best teachers available
of their disciplines, and of publications which set
the highest standard in both content and design

Mindfulness that the purpose of teaching is to enable
students to apply in their own lives that which they learn

To make Temenos known to all those who may benefit
from its work

Reminding ourselves and those we teach
to look up and not down

Governance of the Temenos Academy itself
in light of the above Principles

FOREWORD

In a conversation that took place at some point in the mid-1990s, Kathleen Raine, Keith Critchlow and Warren Kenton discussed the desirability of a set of aims to guide the work of the Temenos Academy. Out of these reflections there emerged ten statements of purpose: framed without explicit reference to any particular tradition or traditions, but – both individually, and in their sequence and interrelationships – embodying universal truths. There was a phase of adjustment and experiment, with one version appearing in 2000 in *Temenos Academy Review* 3; but at length the ten Principles crystallized in the form in which (for instance) they are now to be found on the Academy's website.

When I first undertook the general editorship of *TAR*, Joseph Milne suggested to me that the ten Principles might be an appropriate subject for an editorial. While I thought that the essential idea was a very valuable one, it seemed to me that so large and many-sided a subject could best be approached gradually. In the event, the exploration of the Principles has provided material for the editorials in nine consecutive issues (*TAR* 9–17, covering the years 2006–2014). Now that the series is complete, it has been suggested to me that it might be useful to publish all of these pieces together.

One of the ideas lying behind the original formulation of the Principles was that there should be a set of values to which all who are attached to Temenos could subscribe. In writing the editorials, my aim has therefore been to unfold what I feel to be already implicit within each of the Principles, rather than simply to put forward opinions of my own. To this end I have in each case consulted friends and colleagues in the Academy, to ascertain whether my understanding was in harmony with theirs. I am grateful for the consistently helpful comments and suggestions that I have received, thanks to which the pieces below are – I think and hope – truly representative, rather than merely idiosyncratic. At the same time, I take personal responsibility for all that I have said and missaid.

The texts that follow are nearly the same as those that appeared in *TAR*; I have however somewhat expanded the references, and have moved these to the end of the book. Except where otherwise noted, translations are my own.

JOHN CAREY

I

Acknowledgement of Divinity

THERE WOULD BE AN OBVIOUS FITTINGNESS in taking, as the subject for an editorial in this journal, the 'Ten Basic Principles' which inspire the work of the Temenos Academy. But while this might be fitting, it is scarcely feasible: to speak of even one of the Principles is more than task enough. And it is of course inevitable that this should be so. Temenos contemplates, and takes its stand upon, those things which are most essential to our humanity, and these are matters which cannot be dealt with in a few easy phrases. The wise have reflected on them for thousands of years, and the springs are as fresh, and as bottomless, as ever.

But even though there can be no question of doing justice to such a theme, it may be useful to put the first of the Principles forward as matter for reflection. It is dauntingly terse: *Acknowledgement of Divinity*. How can we best seek to understand these words, and to act upon them?

What do we mean by 'Divinity'? Any answer, if it is to be adequate to the full range of Temenos's concerns – or if, more vitally, it is properly to reflect the whole of the human quest for the sacred – must be broad and flexible. It should comprehend every vision of the Divine, from the single God of the Abrahamic religions to the in-numerable living presences revered by the shamans of the Arctic or the wanderers of the Australian outback. More challenging still, it must not only be able to accommodate all of the varieties of theism, but also such teachings as that of Buddhism, for which the ultimate Reality is a sublime Emptiness; or of Taoism, for which it is that principle of harmonious balance which governs the totality of things. Here too there are, or may be, 'gods': but they, like ourselves, are only incomplete reflections of the Ultimate.

At no time within the reach of our history have the peoples of all the world been able to know so much about each other as now: never before, so far as we are aware, has the inexhaustible multiplicity of human belief been so dizzyingly apparent. Confronted with such a kaleidoscope of visions, can a word like 'Divinity' have any single or coherent meaning? As we consider the problem, there are at any rate some pitfalls that can be avoided.

It might seem natural to understand this diversity in terms of the contrasts between distinct religions. But such a view ignores more than it explains. I wonder whether the differences between one and another are, in the end, any more profound than those which can be found *within* any fully developed tradition. How easy would it be, if the clues of name and language were withheld, to recognise the identity of the Zeus of Plotinus with the Zeus of some Arcadian shrine? The palpable God who invited Thomas to reach into His violated flesh is the same as the No-Thing, beyond every name and beyond our conception of being itself, which Dionysius could only describe in terms of 'dazzling darkness'. In India, Śaṅkara the philosopher followed the way of knowledge toward the Nameless, while Śaṅkara the devotee is said to have followed the way of love, in search of the immortal Flute-Player. The rabbis too have placed the Lord beyond any possibility of qualification, and yet the *Zohar* undertakes to count the hairs of His beard. All of us can think of further examples. I am not insinuating that, within the framework of any given theology, such manifold conceptions cannot be integrated. What does seem to be undeniable, however, is that the richness of the spiritual imagination cannot be limited by unitary formulae.

And yet the mind and heart crave unity. With a profound insight, we sense that the Truth is ultimately One, that there is a single Reality toward which the whole basis of our nature yearns. How are we to find it, amid innumerable prophecies and doctrines?

Many have tried to cut the Gordian knot by deciding that only a single religion, or a single sect, possesses the truth, while all other beliefs are deluded if not indeed positively evil. For me, this attitude is most memorably exemplified in *The Song of Roland*'s bald assertion that 'pagans are wrong and Christians are right'[1] – but of course the sentiment is not limited to Christianity, or to the Middle Ages. At the same time, many voices from many traditions have spoken out against such narrowness. Unanswerable in their mysteriousness are God's words in the Qur'ān:

> For each we have appointed a divine law and a traced-out way. Had Allah willed He could have made you one community. But that He may try you by that which He hath given you (He hath made you as ye are). So vie one with another in good works. Unto Allah ye will all return, and He will then inform you of that wherein ye differ.[2]

More benign, and to many minds more seductive, is the attempt to find unity through inclusion rather than through exclusion: the quest for a core which is common to the doctrines (or to a selection of the doctrines) of all religions (or of a selection of all religions). It has been suggested that this core represents a primordial revelation of which the 'great religions' are all reflections: by comparing traditions with one another, and by observing the ideas which they share, we can accordingly find our way back to that revelation's original purity.

We must tread carefully here. It is indeed the case that very different traditions exhibit strikingly similar symbols, or doctrines, or types of spiritual experience. And that they do so is very important: such confluences open up precious opportunities for mutual understanding – and surely also, at some deeper level, they do reflect aspects of that transcendent realm toward which it is our highest destiny to strive. These analogies are persuasive signs that the various religions are, in Ananda Coomaraswamy's phrase, 'paths that lead to the same summit': facets of a Wisdom which, ever flashing forth afresh at different times and places, can with justice be called a 'perennial philosophy'.

But their sharing of a single goal does not by any means mean that the autonomous integrity of these paths can be disregarded. Each tradition has grown over generations, or centuries, or millennia: its constituents, even if they can be to some extent compared with what we find elsewhere, belong to it like the bones in a body or the fruit on a tree. If we say that one of the 'stations' of a Sufi is 'the same thing' as a state experienced by a Buddhist or Christian contemplative, and if we then go on to try to fit the paths of these different mystics onto a single template, we are not recovering a primeval truth but only gluing together a more or less lifeless pastiche of our own devising. It should not require much reflection to see what arrogance is entailed in the notion that such sages as Eckhart and Suhrawardī and Nāgārjuna had only a partial grasp of truths whose totality can be recovered by the modern comparatist.

All of this brings us back to the recalcitrance of our first question. What is 'Divinity'? Is there, indeed, a meaningful definition which can include the spirits of tree and hill, and also the sky-like vastness of the Buddha-nature?

The answer which I am inclined to hazard – although I am sure that fault can be found with it – would be that Divinity is the invisible, eternal foundation of the perishing transient world which floods our senses. Behind or beneath or above or beyond or within the things which we see is Something (or Someone) else: wholly Other than the bewildering circus of temporal phenomena, and yet the ground without which that circus could not exist. The worshipper of the horned god of the river discerned the vitality of an undying intelligence under the veil of the hurrying water. Blake looking at the sun saw Divinity when he perceived, instead of 'a round Disk of fire somewhat like a Guinea', 'an Innumerable company of the Heavenly host crying Holy Holy Holy is the Lord God Almighty'.[3] The Buddhist's gaze pierces beyond a wheeling universe in which all is conditioned by suffering and loss, by yearning and fear, and sees an unbounded realm of changelessness and clarity.

One does not need to believe in God in order to believe in this Reality; but I wonder whether anyone who does not believe in this Reality can truly believe in God.

Kathleen Raine gave beautiful expression to the balance between immanence and transcendence, to the paradox of an Ultimate which is never 'this' yet always *here*, when she spoke in her later poetry of 'the Presence' which is also 'Mystery'. Nothing is closer to us: 'Never have you not been/Here and now in every now and here'.[4] And yet our sensings of it are always of something which escapes us even as it blesses us:

> Here on this threshold of mystery
> Unknown, unknowable as this
> Familiar commonplace where light from fiat falls
> I in ignorance praise
> This veil that is the holy face it veils.[5]

When the Principles were first formulated, in the third issue of this review, the first of them had a somewhat different form: it was *Acknowledgement of the holiness of Divinity, which is beyond all, yet accessible to each.* I feel that I have already gone well out of my depth; and I will fare no better if I make any attempt at defining holiness. But there are a few things which I will make bold to try to say.

'Holy', and the words which serve as its equivalents in other languages, are used of the Ultimate beyond all worlds: long before Blake's vision of the sun, Isaiah had heard *Qâdosh, qâdosh, qâdosh* being chanted by seraphim before the throne of the Lord.[6] But the quality of holiness, although native to the eternal country, also permeates our world of time. There are holy days and holy places, holy trees and beasts and people, holy words and holy gestures, holy water and wine and bread. To say that Divinity is holy is to say that, in some sense, it is all around us. In Blake's words, no less inspiring because they are so familiar, 'every thing that lives is holy.'[7]

To speak of holiness, therefore, is to speak of responsibility. In a world which is full of holy beings, of holy states and seasons, we are to cherish and revere that sanctity, to abstain from desecration. And besides *keeping* things holy, we can also *make* them holy: this is perhaps the primary function of the inspired Imagination.

Most important of all, it is our destiny to become holy ourselves, or rather to realise the holiness which is already our essential nature. (It is, of course, a part of our freedom that we will not necessarily fulfil

7

this destiny.) In so far as we do this, we too participate in Divinity. When the Upanishads speak of the Self hidden within the heart, or the Zoroastrian scriptures of the *fravashis* which constitute Ahura Mazda's presence in all creatures, they point to the possibility of such participation. The same meaning has been found in the statement that the protoplast in the Garden was shaped in God's 'image and likeness'; and in the Psalmist's enigmatic words, 'I have said, ye are gods.'[8]

It may be fair to say that Divinity, in so far as it is Mystery, is 'beyond all'; while in so far as it is Presence it is 'accessible to each'. The top of the ladder rises infinitely beyond our sight, but its rungs are in our hands and under our feet. More than that: the ladder is ourselves. Using another image, Angelus Silesius wrote:

> *Ich bin ein Berg in Gott*
> *und muß mich selber steigen,*
> *daferne Gott mir soll*
> *sein liebes Antlitz zeigen.*[9]

'I am a mountain in God, and I must climb myself in order that God may show me His dear face.' We ourselves are that mountain in the wilderness at whose foot we cower, its summit hidden in dark clouds.

In all of this I have not mentioned one obvious fact: that we live in times which are, to an extent which the world may not have seen before, alienated from the very ideas of Divinity and of holiness. For very many in our society, and perhaps for most of those who govern and educate us, any talk of such things is mere nonsense and delusion. We are all familiar with this positivist consensus, and with the price which the world is paying for it: I shall not embark on any counter-polemic here. It must be said, however, that on this point there is not for Temenos any possibility of compromise. We must each bear witness to Reality, to the extent that we are capable. We cannot make any better beginning than to seek its presence in ourselves.

II

*Love of wisdom, as the essential basis
of civilization*

III

Spiritual vision, as the life-breath of civilization

WHAT IS CIVILIZATION? When Ananda Coomaraswamy chose that question as the title for an essay, his own first response was to dig back to the word's Indo-European root.[10] I shall begin more slowly, and more prosaically, with the Latin terms to which it is most closely and obviously akin. 'Civilization' is the act or process of rendering someone or something *civilis* or 'civil', 'civility' in turn being the quality of the *civis*, the 'citizen'. The *civis* is the inhabitant of the *civitas*, or 'city'. A naively etymological answer to our question could, then, be that 'civilization' is what brings folk to live in cities. Such a definition would strike many of us nowadays as being ironic, if not indeed absurd – and almost anyone, I think, would feel that it required qualification. It is worthwhile to reflect on why this should be so. Our cities are, after all, full of the benefits of civilization: why is it that they themselves seem only intermittently civilized? Why have we ceased to expect that the residents of cities will be notable for their civility? Why has the word 'urban' come to have such different connotations from 'urbane' – and why, indeed, is the latter adjective on its way to becoming obsolete?

Evidently, our idea of what cities are has changed. Whatever actuality there ever was in the ideal represented by *civis* and its derivatives, our experience has taken us in another direction. The roots of this disenchantment lie a long way back. Side by side with the archetype of the heavenly city, 'prepared as a bride adorned for her husband', there seems always to have existed the dystopian vision of the city built by men in God's despite. This image has haunted the Abrahamic traditions ever since the first city in the world was reared by the blood-stained hands of Cain. (And is it only a coincidence that Rome too was said to have been founded by a fratricide?) Thence the shadow spread to Babel and Babylon, to Sodom and Gomorrah, to the prison cities of Egypt, to Nineveh, to ʿIram of the many pillars. Jerusalem herself is red with the blood of the prophets, and Jesus wept at his foreknowledge of her destruction. Dante found no blessed cities in Purgatory or Paradise; but he did come to Dis, with its smouldering iron walls and 'grim citizens', and he saw in the eighth circle things which reminded him of Rome and Venice.[11]

The great Christian theorist of the two cities was Augustine: his *City of God* traces their divided history back to the first dissension among the angels, and contrasts the earthly city with that heavenly one – of which it is both the enemy and the symbol – which 'wanders in exile . . . in this rush of time'.[12] More chillingly prescient is Giambattista Vico's evocation of the fate of those city-dwellers for whom all the lights of the spirit have gone out:

> . . . No matter how great the throng and press of their bodies, they live like wild beasts in a deep solitude of spirit and will, scarcely any two being able to agree since each follows his own pleasure or caprice . . .. They shall turn their cities into forests, and the forests into dens and lairs of men.[13]

Following these thoughts through to their conclusion, C. S. Lewis in *The Great Divorce* imagined the whole of Hell as a vast grey city, sprawling endlessly outward without pattern or centre, its expansion driven by the mutual antipathy of its inhabitants.

To keep from sliding into the concrete jungle, into Vico's 'dens and lairs of men', it is clear that we must seek to live in *community*. There can be no civility, or civilization, without mutual regard. The Psalmist praises Jerusalem as being 'builded as a city that is compact together';[14] and Protagoras, relating to Socrates his myth of the origin of cities, describes how Hermes imparted to mankind 'respect and fairness',[15] qualities without which no cities can exist at all. Here we come close to the conception that citizenship is essential to full

our minds are not limited by a single lifetime

humanity – and indeed, as Coomaraswamy noted, the *Atharva Veda* derives the Sanskrit word for 'person' (*puruṣa*) from the word for 'city' (*pura*).[16]

But what sort of community is truly constitutive of civilization? Concern for one another, a shared purpose, a harmonious collective life, are all noble and deeply precious, but they are not exclusively human – we can admire such qualities in a hive of bees, a flock of penguins, or a pack of wolves. What distinguishes the human community – and what is, accordingly, the basis of the true city – is its freedom from the shackles of immediacy. Our minds are not limited by a single season, or a single lifetime. As a community, we have inherited the memories of our ancestors, and it is as their representatives that we and our children advance into the riddle of the future.

Everything that we think of as civilization – our sense of who we are, our ideas of morality and decorum, the innumerable fruits of skill and inspiration to which we turn for beauty or for enlightenment – all this belongs to a fabric that unites us, layer upon layer, with the whole of the inhabited past. Only humans possess this, and in the end we cannot live without it. G. K. Chesterton says this vigorously in his essay 'The Ethics of Elfland':

> I have never been able to understand where people got the idea that democracy was in some way opposed to tradition. It is obvious that tradition is only democracy extended through time . . . .. Tradition means giving votes to the most obscure of all classes, our ancestors. It is the democracy of the dead. Tradition refuses to submit to the small and arrogant minority of those who merely happen to be walking about.[17]

Civilization and tradition seem, therefore, to be versions of one another.

I hope to write more about tradition on another occasion. At present, however, armed with these tentative reflections on the theme of civilization, I want to turn to the second and third of the ten Principles which inspire the work of Temenos:

Love of wisdom, as the essential basis of civilization
Spiritual vision, as the life-breath of civilization

What are these faculties, and how can we best nurture them?

'Love of wisdom' is of course the original meaning of the Greek word *philosophia*. It was Pythagoras, according to a tradition which seems to find its earliest attestation in the writings of Cicero, who first called himself a *philosophos*, not presuming to make the bolder claim that he was wise. Here he set a good example. But, in our own lack of wisdom, can we even say what it is that we seek to love?

Often images are more eloquent than definitions; and one of the most radiant images of what I am trying to examine is afforded by the Book of Proverbs. Here it is Wisdom herself who speaks to us. Although the text does not belong to the earliest strata of the Hebrew canon it reflects ancient perceptions, which can be compared with portrayals of the goddess Truth in the scriptures of pharaonic Egypt:

The Lord possessed me in the beginning of His way, before His works of old.

I was set up from everlasting, from the beginning, or ever the earth was.

When there were no depths, I was brought forth; when there were no fountains abounding with water.

Before the mountains were settled, before the hills was I brought forth:

While as yet He had not made the earth, nor the fields, nor the highest part of the dust of the world.

When He prepared the heavens, I was there: when He set a compass upon the face of the depth:

When He established the clouds above: when He strengthened the fountains of the deep:

When He gave to the sea His decree, that the waters should not pass His commandment: when He appointed the foundations of the earth:

Then I was by Him, as one brought up with Him: and I was daily His light, rejoicing always before Him:

Rejoicing in the habitable part of His earth; and my delights were with the sons of men.

Now therefore hearken unto me, O ye children: for blessed are they that keep my ways.[18]

Wisdom, existing since before time's beginning, witnessing the shaping and establishing of the universe, is a principle of cosmic order. But Wisdom is also she whose delights are with the sons of men, she who seeks to render her children blessed through her teachings. She exists beyond all worlds and yet, when our hearts are open, she also moves among us.

When we think of wisdom sharing God's throne at the world's creation, we apprehend its transcendent unity. But what is unitary in principle is endlessly diverse in application. How could it be otherwise, if wisdom indeed governs the infinite complexity of the natural world, and can indeed offer us guidance in the bewildering particularities of our always-surprising lives? The desire to impose abstractions and generalizations upon the texture of existence has little to do with the love of wisdom. As Blake observed, 'General Knowledge is Remote Knowledge; it is in Particulars that Wisdom consists & Happiness too'.[19] Nor can anyone dictate where wisdom is to be found: in the words of a *hadīth*, it is the 'stray camel of the believer', who is entitled to claim it no matter how strange may be the place to which it has wandered.

That wisdom both turns the stars and guides the heart, and that the just city is interdependent with a stable world, are ideas found already in the oldest sources. The *Rig Veda* says that 'the rivers pour forth justice, the sun has spread out truth',[20] while Homer speaks of

> . . . a blameless king, fearing the gods and holding sway over many strong men. He upholds fair dealing, and the black earth bears wheat and barley, and the trees are heavy with fruit. The sheep give birth in due season, and the sea provides fish, on account of his good rule; and his subjects thrive because of him.[21]

Such a conception gives a deeper resonance to the pronouncement that love of wisdom is the basis of civilization; and this is of course especially the case in our own troubled times. What, in our culture, is the relationship between human wisdom and the cycles of nature? Job says that God found wisdom 'when He made a decree for the rain, and a way for the lightning of the thunder: Then did He see it, and declare it; He prepared it, yea, and searched it out'.[22] What should we 'see' and 'declare' as the ice melts and the seas rise, as floods and droughts and hurricanes grow fiercer and more frequent? What can we claim for our civilization?

Toward the end of the Book of Proverbs, in a section attributed to King Solomon, there stands the statement 'Where there is no vision, the people perish'.[23] The Hebrew word translated as 'vision' is *ḥāzôn*: it designates that which God makes known to His prophets, and also their ability to hear and to see the things which He reveals to them. In effect, and within the context of a single revealed tradition, the words of Solomon enunciate our third Principle.

In seeking to find a way in which to speak of wisdom, I turned to symbolic language. With 'spiritual vision', symbolism is already present in the phrase itself. The visionary 'sees', but does so with what Henry Corbin called 'eyes of fire' rather than with the eye of flesh. Such vision, as Blake taught, does not stop with physical appearances: it penetrates to the 'Permanent Realities of Every Thing which we see reflected in this Vegetable Glass of Nature'.[24]

Wisdom shows us how we should live in the world; vision points beyond it. We require both in order to be fully ourselves. If 'every thing that lives is holy' then we need such vision, again and again, to reveal to us and recall to us the Source of all life and holiness. If our true home and happiness are beyond the cycles of embodied time, then we must have light for our feet upon the road – flashing, as Śāntideva says of 'enlightened awareness' or *bodhicitta*, like lightning out of the black clouds of the night.[25]

Vision discloses other worlds to us: heavens and hells; the chariot and its creatures above the river Chebar; emerald cities upon the mountain of Qāf at the world's rim; meticulously mapped provinces of darkness traversed each night by the sun-god Re; the undying Plain of Delights, which the medieval Irish thought that they might glimpse if only they could shake from their eyes the 'darkness of Adam's sin'.[26]

Where are these places? In the words of one of their inhabitants, they are 'maybe near, maybe far':[27] even if they are in some sense 'elsewhere', that 'elsewhere' is not spatially separate from 'here'. If 'vision' is only a metaphor, then 'beyond' is another. The Otherworld is not an alternative to the world we know, an escapist or dualist fantasy: on the contrary, it is nothing else than its timeless essence. Entering it, we take our first steps into the country of the Real. Its mysteries are hidden not so much behind the surfaces of things as behind the surfaces of our own perceptions of them. And anything can twitch the veil aside (although, for most of us, it is back in place again before we are aware that anything has happened): the crazy challenge of a *koan*, the beauty of a hovering bird, light glinting off a pewter dish.

Those who have sought to cultivate the faculty of vision have tended to observe firm discipline: silence and solitude, prayer and fasting, the detaching of the mind from yearnings and preoccupations. It is when we are quiet that we can best hear, when we gaze into the open that we can see the farthest. From this perspective, it is evident that the way in which we now live is the enemy of vision. It is not merely that we are under constant pressure to indulge our cravings and to acquire more possessions, not merely that the tempo of anxieties and distractions grows ever faster and more insistent. At any time in the course of the last few centuries it would have been possible to make such complaints (or excuses) as these. But the technical advances of our own day have brought something further: our imagination itself, the very organ of vision, is now being bombarded and colonized by such a flood of stimuli as humanity has never before experienced. In this blaring phantasmagoria, who can hope to hear the 'still small voice' which spoke to Elijah in his cave in the wilderness?

This is a problem which should be taken seriously. We are in danger of allowing a part of ourselves to atrophy, and of losing a faculty on which we depend for far more than we know. If it were ever to wither away entirely, who is to say that we would not perish?

Our cultural situation is perilous, but it is not matter for despair. Again and again throughout the ages, men and women have felt their world grow stale with selfishness and sour with vice: the old words have rung hollow, the old images have become dead encumbrances blocking out the light. But again and again – whether to imperial Rome, crushed beneath its own weight and dreaming of primitive virtue; or to the precarious constructions of late Scholasticism, spun like intricate webs across a gulf of plague and war; or to the complacent simplifications of the Enlightenment; or to the manic depredations of the Industrial Revolution – the Spirit has returned, speaking with the voices of Plotinus and Eckhart and Novalis and Blake. The words of Christ to Nicodemus trace the thread of our inmost history:

> That which is born of the flesh is flesh; and that which is born of the Spirit is spirit. Marvel not that I said unto thee, Ye must be born again. The wind bloweth where it listeth, and thou hearest the sound thereof, but canst not tell whence it cometh, and whither it goeth: so is everyone that is born of the Spirit.[28]

In every time and place, and for every soul, there is the need for a new birth. This is our most fundamental calling as individuals: but we are also summoned as a community. While mortality endures, there will never be an end to the task which belongs to all of us: the building of our true city, cradled in the arms of our mother Wisdom and incandescent with invisible fire.

IV

Maintenance of the revered traditions of mankind

V

Understanding of tradition as continual renewal

SOMETIMES THE STUDY OF A WORD'S BACKGROUND reveals a sacred basis, which has been blunted and obscured over time. This is not the case with the word 'tradition'. The Latin *traditio* means simply a 'handing over' of any kind, not excluding the handing over of property in commercial transactions, or indeed the various sorts of 'handing over' which are involved in acts of betrayal. Our words 'treason' and 'traitor' both go back to the verb *trado* from which *traditio* derives.

In Greek, the same range of meanings can be seen in the noun *paradosis* and the verb *paradidōmi*: it is the latter which is used in the Gospels to describe the treachery of Judas. Jesus, on the only occasion when he is said to have spoken of *paradosis*, used the word to mean 'tradition' – but he did so while referring, in harsh condemnation, to the traditions of the Pharisees. 'Abandoning God's command, you hold fast to the traditions of men'.[29] Paul too, as he remembered the bloodthirsty self-righteousness which had preceded the shock of his enlightenment, spoke remorsefully of having persecuted God's followers out of zeal for 'the traditions of my fathers';[30] and when Krishna alluded to those who, 'disputing the letter of the Vedas', assert that 'There is nothing else than this',[31] he was describing similar attitudes in ancient India.

The fourth of the ten Principles which guide the work of Temenos enjoins upon us the *maintenance of the revered traditions of mankind*. It is salutary, then, to observe how often the scriptures which stand at the heart of those traditions warn us of the ease with which tradition itself can lead us astray. We cannot simply declare our allegiance to 'tradition', and leave it at that. We must explain ourselves; and we must, each for himself or herself, question ourselves beforehand.

In an illuminating discussion of 'The Meaning and Necessity of Sacred Tradition', Philip Sherrard defined 'sacred tradition in the highest sense' as 'the preservation and handing down of a method of contemplation'.[32] The source of such a tradition is revelation: when we submit to this revelation, and thereby accept the authority of the tradition's mediators, we renounce 'our self-centred individualism and the ego-consciousness that goes with it'.[33] This liberating humility is essential.

> Although we may think that formal attachment to the discipline of a particular sacred tradition is unnecessary because the Spirit blows where it wills and so can inspire and illumine those not attached to such a tradition just as well as, or even better than, those who are so attached, it is surely presumption and spiritual pride (the least spiritual of characteristics, whose presence in a person would in any case preclude any visitation by the Spirit) to imagine that the Spirit will choose us for special and privileged attention when we have already rejected or scorned perfectly good and well-tried ways through which the Spirit has already chosen to manifest His influence.[34]

Inasmuch as a sacred tradition is not simply a collection of ideas, but a path leading to transformation, it comprises two equally fundamental aspects: *gnosis*, or revealed knowledge; and the *discipline* whereby one conforms one's life to the truth which has been revealed. The soundness of these observations is manifest in the wisdom, sanctity and beauty which have flourished wherever and whenever a spiritual tradition has been maintained in its integrity. But there have of course, repeatedly, been times and places which have lacked such guidance; while in our own age the radically anti-traditional vision which has come to dominate the West is aggressively extending itself throughout the remainder of the globe. How can we best endeavour to reconnect ourselves to the ancient ways – if, indeed, it is not now too late to do so?

Many of the sacred traditions are living still. To seek them out, to support them insofar as we are able, to find one or another to which we can entrust our lives – these are goals which Temenos exists to further. But this is not all; nor is it even, in Kathleen Raine's view, quite enough. In her challenging essay 'Revisioning the Sacred for our Time', she spoke of the sacred traditions as 'records of adventures into the unknown regions of the inner worlds'; at the same time, however, she held that 'we are most unlikely . . . to discover the inner realities through the old forms'.[35] Amid the seismic changes which are assailing every aspect of our mental and social life, it may be that the spiritual path 'can no longer be one or another of the world-religions with a received pantheon of sacred figures, but a culture based on knowledge of the archetypes themselves'.[36]

A new culture of the spiritual order – that is to say of the world of the sacred – means, certainly, that we can no longer give an absolute attachment to any 'religion', since all religions are seen to be relative. But it may be that through the opening of those inner worlds, the universe to which all pantheons and sacred stories are native, we will come to a truer understanding of the import and sacredness of the persons and sacred stories of our own and other religions.[37]

It will be evident that there is a discrepancy between this position and that taken by Philip Sherrard; similar disagreement, fruitfully provocative, is reflected later in this issue.[38]

Rather than turn the concept of sacred tradition into a battleground, we can reflect that this concept is characterized, or indeed defined, by an inherent tension. Each sacred tradition arises from the reflection of some facet of the Timeless in the stream of Time. There is always the possibility – with the passage of the generations, perhaps the growing likelihood – that the mortal limitations of the transmitters may veil or eclipse the transcendent radiance of the Origin. But even if the teachings are faithfully conveyed, we are left with the paradox of a message which purports to liberate us from the very Time which is its vehicle. Votaries of a sacred tradition can be true to what they have received from the past only if, on another level, the past means nothing to them.

It is in these terms that we can approach the fifth of our Principles: the *understanding of tradition as continual renewal*. The perennial teachings have lost their truth if that truth lies elsewhere than in this moment, and in the choices which belong to each of us: in the words of the *Mahābhārata*, 'What is not here, is not anywhere'.[39] The Buddha said: 'It is you who must make the effort. The Great of the past only show the way'.[40] Years before the founding of the Academy, Kathleen Raine expressed the essence of the fifth Principle more fully when she stated that 'sacred tradition is not a continuation of the past, but a continual renewal of the vision of eternal reality'.[41]

Whenever there is a need for balance, there will be differences of interpretation; and, since balance is always needful, we will always have such differences. Where we decide to stand is the responsibility of each of us individually. But I think that there are some things on which all who have felt the call of Temenos will agree. The truths revealed to our ancestors have born fruit in teachings and images and forms of life which are essential both to our humanity and to our relationship with the Real: such traditions are the immaterial treasures of the world, deserving all the reverence and dedication of which we are capable. But, precisely because of what they are, they must live within us if they are to live at all – otherwise they will decay and breed vermin, like the manna hoarded in the wilderness. 'Their authority' (to quote Kathleen Raine again) 'comes not from history or ecclesiastical authority, but from within, from a timeless order'.[42]

This constitutes a challenge, for it asks everything of us. (Then again, what is the worth of an ideal which asks for less?) But also, in an age in which Time may appear to be debasing or destroying all that is precious, it is a comfort to reflect that the chances of Time have nothing to do with what is most precious of all. As Philip Sherrard also wrote,

> . . . we can take heart in the knowledge that the realities of which our world appears to be so dispossessed are not and never can be dead and gone; and that if we do no more than lament their absence then what we condone is our own failure to allow them

to manifest their presence and animate our lives and works. Both man and nature possess an ineradicable capacity for self-renewal. We have but to shift our gaze, to alter the focus of our attention, and the waters will be cleansed, the ancient springs will flow again.[43]

The symbol of the spring, existing only insofar as it brings into our daylight the sparkling life-blood of its Source, expresses the nature of tradition immeasurably better than any words of mine.

VI (i)

The provision of teaching by the best teachers
available of their disciplines . . .

THE SIXTH OF THE TEN PRINCIPLES that inspire the work of our Academy calls for *the provision of teaching by the best teachers available of their disciplines, and of publications which set the highest standard in both content and design.* This is a formidable charge, and we cannot be confident that we will always fulfil it; but it is a goal which well deserves our greatest efforts. This goal, and these efforts, comprise much of what is most essential to the Temenos Academy, for they embody our commitment to *scholarship* and to *craftsmanship*. Two enormous themes; in what follows here, I shall only venture to treat of the first.

Has scholarship in fact any necessary connection with the fundamental concerns of Temenos – with the Imagination and the sacred? One could easily find reasons for doubting it. All too often, the pursuit of knowledge becomes a mechanical amassing and sifting of information, in which any initial sense of wonder dwindles into the restlessness of a merely cerebral curiosity, or into simple vanity and ambition. Analysis, when it seeks understanding through reduction and dissection, excludes by its very methods the possibility that anything can be higher than the mind of the investigator, and sees no task for reason beyond the abolition of mystery. In the universities, and in the wider world of the professionally clever, it can seem that the arrogance of a secular rationalism takes it virtually for granted that materialism, scepticism, iconoclasm and the rejection of tradition are the attributes of every educated person.

Studying a thing can be a substitute for, if not indeed a protection against, any true encounter with what is studied. Thus the Sufi sage

Jāmī observed that 'the heir of the Prophet is the one who follows the Prophet in his dealings, not the one who blackens the face of paper';[44] while for Pascal 'an idol is made out of truth itself; for apart from love truth is not God. It is His image, and an idol which one need not love or worship'.[45]

How well these arrows strike their mark I know from myself: from my own preoccupations, prevarications and failures. A concern with learning can be a formidable obstacle to the search for inner stillness and simplicity, and to the insights which only such stillness and simplicity can bestow.

But while the justice in all of this must be acknowledged, demonizing scholarship is not the answer. The Way will not be found by undisciplined thinking – nor by that literalism which, arrogating to itself the name of faith, seeks to hedge in and regiment the Light. The idea that intellectual rigour and spiritual search are fundamentally incompatible can have various sources: the dismissiveness of an academic establishment for which everything outside its own ambit is delusion and fantasy; the frustrated alienation experienced by those who have found no nourishment in the universities; the desire to protect one's own understanding of a revelation (as distinct from that revelation itself) from whatever may seem to threaten it. But to conclude from such attitudes that there really *is* a breach between reason and the holy is to embrace precisely those prejudices which Temenos is called upon to challenge. And it is a fallacy: scholarship in the service of the spirit can, and should, be even stricter in its demands than a scholarship bounded by the findings of empiricism.

In fact, of course, every ensouled tradition has cherished knowledge and the search for knowledge: it is only when tradition ossifies into traditionalism that learning comes to be at odds with inspiration. The divinity within the breast of Socrates taught him no holier duty than a perpetual readiness to question. In our times, and especially in the Anglo-American sphere, the word 'philosophy' has a very specific – some would say narrow – application; but formerly it was used of every branch of study. And the original meaning of 'philosophy' is 'love of Wisdom': scholarship, and science, were held to be a kind of love.

It is in this spirit that the great Platonist teacher Thierry of Chartres, one of whose treatises is translated in this issue, wrote in the preface to his *Heptateuchon*:

> Inasmuch as there are two principal instruments of philosophizing, namely intellect and its interpretation, and intellect illuminates the *quadrivium* [i.e., arithmetic, geometry, astronomy and music], while its elegant, reasonable and ornamented interpretation ministers to the *trivium* [i.e., grammar, rhetoric and dialectic], it is plain that the seven liberal arts are the sole and singular instrument of all philosophy. For philosophy is the love of Wisdom; while Wisdom is the undivided comprehension of the Truth of the things that are, which no one can touch even a little if he has not loved it (*quam nullus uel parum adipiscitur nisi amauerit*). Therefore no one is wise unless he be a philosopher.[46]

And some three hundred years earlier, when the Pope's librarian marvelled at Eriugena's erudite command of Greek, he surmised that 'Love was his schoolmistress' (*hunc magistra Caritas docuit*).[47]

Pascal, as we have seen, held that 'apart from love truth is not God': may we not go a step further, and say that apart from love truth is not even truth? Indeed, no real scholarship can exist without a sort of love, for it is in love that one opens oneself to the other. A lover cannot hope truly to encounter the beloved without an attention so acute, so urgent, that the self is forgotten. Understanding comes only in silence, a stilling of all inner chatter in order to hear another voice. And love, as long as it endures, is an unending journey of discovery. To impose our own projections on the object of our devotion is idolatry – it is not love. And with true scholarship, and true science, it is no different.

Despite the impatience of those who trust only their own enraptured instincts, a scrupulous attention to investigative method is more needful now than it has ever been before. For we live amid the wreckage of our own tradition, and the wrecking of innumerable others: if we look for guidance, much of it now lies in the past. And how can we attend to the teachings of the dead? Only by learning their languages, by becoming acquainted with their symbols, by finding our way back into their history. The Romantics knew this. It belongs to the myopia of our times that we choose to forget how much we owe, not only to their poetry, but also to their scholarship.

But although the essence of scholarship is wholly in harmony with the Truth which it serves, there can be no question that it is otherwise with much scholarship as it is practised. Whether directly or indirectly, our institutions of learning collectively deny the importance or indeed the reality of That for whose sake Temenos exists. When we speak of 'the best teachers', therefore, we mean something very different from the lions of academe. We seek a rarer breed: men and women who, whether inside or outside the universities, are true to the highest intellectual standards without submitting to that modern pride which ignores the Presence, and resists the Mystery.

VI (ii)

. . . and of publications which set the highest standard in both content and design

THE SIXTH OF THE PRINCIPLES which guide the work of the Temenos Academy affirms that we are committed to providing *publications which set the highest standard in both content and design*. This twofold ideal has been fundamental to the Academy since its inception, and the same held true for the review *Temenos* which preceded it. Thus Kathleen Raine, in the flyer which announced the publication of *Temenos* 6 in 1985, wrote that

> our printing costs are high; and believing as we do that the making of a book is itself an art we have no wish to betray those values we stand for by lowering standards of production any more than that of our contents.

Such stringency could easily be regarded as mere aestheticism. If there is something which it is important to communicate, surely it is the message which is essential, not the vehicle – and, if resources are limited, surely these should be devoted to disseminating that message as widely as possible, not to a perfectionist preoccupation with paper, type and binding. Nowadays, indeed, it could be asked whether there is any longer any point at all in a printed journal: increasingly, whatever information matters travels through the Internet.

I suspect that many readers of this journal are, like myself, moved by sentiment or instinct to react against such utilitarianism. But while this is a healthy reaction, we should not allow it to close the question; for more than sentiment and instinct is at stake. What might seem to be no more than a matter of taste is in fact bound up with issues basic to the modernist paradigm.

I am thinking here of the dualism of Descartes: his doctrine that mind and matter differ so utterly from one another that there can be no contact between them. We have no shared being with the world, or with anything material – not even with our own bodies. In the lines which lead up to the formulation of his famous axiom 'Je pense donc je suis', Descartes recorded his conviction that he was

> a substance whose entire essence or nature is nothing except to think, and which has no need of any place in order to be, nor does it depend on any material thing. Accordingly, this 'I', that is to say the mind, by which I am and which I am, is entirely distinct from the body . . ..[48]

Matter, alien and inanimate, can be at best an *instrument* of thought – the more nakedly and uncomplicatedly so, from this point of view, the better.

This philosophical position, which has of course played a crucial part in the emergence of modern rationalism, has also had direct practical consequences in determining how we regard the things which surround us, the things which we use and make. Devoid of any connection with the world of thought which is the realm of the 'I', these things are seen to lack any inherent value or meaning, except insofar as they function to our benefit. The entire sphere of the made is only, to use Le Corbusier's famous definition of a house, a 'machine for living in'.

The traditions which have inspired Temenos see the world in a wholly different light. Whatever it may be – concrete, or illusory, or somehow both – the universe of matter is a reflection, a manifestation, of the unchanging kingdom of the spirit. Transcendent and immanent are bound together; and what joins them is the realm of soul, which is the Imagination. It is through Imagination that the cosmos came into being; and it is through Imagination that the phenomenal world can be made transparent, a window onto the invisible glory of Reality.

Mortal making is itself an image of the making which is the origin of the world. It is perhaps most essentially as makers that we are, as

Genesis tells us, formed in the likeness of our Creator. And in every act of making we are called upon to follow that primordial example, embodying and revealing the True.

In his editorial for *Temenos 6*, Brian Keeble has written that

a thing wrought to the perfection of its being is an affirmation of the unity and wholeness of Being itself. For, by implication, when a thing is well and truly made some reverberation of that thing's archetypal perfection has taken place and thus some sanctity has been brought down into human life.[49]

Among the innumerable works of human hands and minds, a book is one of the most obvious vehicles of revelation – especially so for the Abrahamic religions, known to Islam as the 'Religions of the Book'. The sublimity of Qur'ānic illumination, like that of the sacred manuscripts of Christianity, testifies to the awareness that a book symbolizes that mystery which is the manifestation of the Unmanifest. As S. H. Nasr says in his essay 'The Spiritual Message of Islamic Calligraphy':

The calamus with which the human hand writes is a direct symbol of that Divine *Qalam* and the calligraphy it traces on paper or parchment an image of that Divine Calligraphy which has written the very reality of all things upon the pages of the cosmic book.[50]

In none of the other works of human artifice, perhaps, is the chasm which Descartes bequeathed to us so palpably bridged; in a book, words and the thoughts which gave them birth take concrete form upon the page.

Temenos has at all times been blessed with designers, calligraphers, typesetters and printers whose skill and dedication render our publications things of beauty. In striving to bear witness through such craftsmanship, we seek no more than to be true to that for whose sake we testify. The ideals which Temenos serves are not merely concepts to be learned about, but realities which we are summoned to make actual. What we make is as much a statement as what we teach – indeed, it is a part of the same thing. In the words of Eric Gill:

> 'Art and religion', we say, and we yoke the two words as though they might not naturally be found together. In fact they cannot be separated. Religion, the word, shorn of all its sectarian associations, means simply the experience of God. Man, the artist, is man experiencing himself as God, collaborating with God in creating, his imagination formative of things and not formed by them. You cannot separate art and religion. The religious man is simply man, and the artist is simply religious man turned workman.[51]

Each of us, in whatever it is we do, can endeavour to enact that mirroring of the heavenly in the earthly which is the recollection of Paradise. This is what human life is meant to be.

VII

*Mindfulness that the purpose of teaching
is to enable students to apply in their own lives
that which they learn*

KATHLEEN RAINE LIKED TO QUOTE A. K. Coomaraswamy's saying that it takes four years to get a first-rate university education, and forty years to get over it. That a deadly seriousness lay behind this quip is apparent from Coomaraswamy's words elsewhere:

> A single generation of English education suffices to break the threads of tradition and to create a nondescript and superficial being deprived of all roots – a sort of intellectual pariah who does not belong to the East or the West, the past or the future.[52]

This was written with specific reference to the exporting of British educational methods to colonial India; but it has a more general application. In the battle for the soul of the world, education is probably the most potent weapon of all. It is in this light that I would like to reflect on the seventh of the Principles that guide the work of the Academy: *Mindfulness that the purpose of teaching is to enable students to apply in their own lives that which they learn.*

What is it that we teach at Temenos? A matter-of-fact answer would be religion, philosophy, literature, art – the familiar stock in trade of the humanities. It is a range of subjects that can be found in the arts faculties of most universities; and it is from the universities that many of our speakers come to us. Temenos could be seen as an outgrowth of the academic establishment, providing educational evenings as one of the cultural amenities of Greater London.

This is doubtless what the Academy represents for some at least of those who attend our lectures and seminars – perhaps, indeed, for some of our speakers as well – and such visitors are welcome on that basis. Our true concern, however, is with something fundamentally different. If all that Temenos purveyed were education in this familiar, innocuous, conventional sense, then it would have failed.

The Temenos Academy differs from most modern schools and universities in its affirmation of the reality and centrality of the Sacred; and many of the texts, teachers and traditions which it studies – more and more of them, it sometimes seems – are difficult or impossible to learn about in conventional institutions. In the address which she delivered at the opening of the Academy, twenty years ago, Kathleen Raine spoke of rediscovering an 'excluded knowledge' which, largely ignored by professional academia, is in fact the life-blood of all that is most precious in our civilization:

> What was at issue was not simply a matter of a few forgotten names but of the whole body of the world's wisdom, the mainstream of an alternative tradition, grounded not in the naïve materialism of a few centuries, but in the 'Perennial Philosophy' in all its branches . . . simply excluded from our Universities as if it did not exist . . . .

This is of great importance, but it is by no means all. The real essence of our endeavour is conveyed in the words with which she went on to qualify the passage which I have just quoted:

> . . . Or, if mentioned, not as the sacred literature of wisdom, but as 'history of ideas' in which students are expected to learn *about*, not to learn *from*, these records of humankind's deepest thought and highest vision.[53]

This is the crucial distinction, involving two entirely different modes of relationship. When we learn *about* someone or something, we are studying an object: our mind's eye could just as well be directed at a culture in a Petri dish or at a reaction in a flask, and what we confront is in Martin Buber's terminology an *it*. But to learn *from* is to sit – at first, perhaps, simply to pray for the privilege of sitting – at the feet of a teacher. And this teacher – whether man or woman or book or painting or tree or star or deity – is a *thou*.

The word 'academy' has had a long and often dreary history, and a good deal of dispiriting baggage has attached itself to its offshoots 'academic' and 'academia'. But the Temenos Academy looks back to the first Academy: the shady park northwest of Athens, sacred to the Arcadian hero Akademos, where Plato discoursed with his disciples. Truth was sought there in dialogue, in relationship: in learning *from*. It is perhaps paradoxical that Plato put all of his teaching into written accounts of conversations – it is as if writing is telling us that writing cannot tell us. This is the paradox of the Gospels also. Behind it is the recognition that wisdom can only be sought in the humility, in the vulnerability, of an encounter.

Plato's conviction that truth is found in the meeting of minds, not in some fixed form of words, finds its most vivid expression in a famous passage in his *Seventh Letter*:

> When each of these things – names and statements, appearances and perceptions – was laboriously compared with the others, examined in friendly discussion, employing questions and answers without envy: then the intellect and mind of each, straining human capacity to the utmost possible, were filled with light. No one seriously concerned with such matters would attempt to replace this process with a written account . . ..[54]

Plato stood on the threshold of a new age of the mind, both exhilarated and troubled by the power of the written word. The generations who have come after have found that books need not by any means be mere passive objects: we can learn from them, argue with them, journey into them, almost as if it is their writers who are there with us. But in such cases the principle is the same: such a book stands for a person, a *thou*.

In these terms, if what we learn does not change us then we have not really learned anything at all. The Buddha warns of this when he compares one who 'speaks many holy words but he speaks and does not' to 'a cowherd who counts the cows of his master'; and again when he speaks of the fool who 'never knows the path of wisdom as the spoon never knows the taste of the soup'.[55] Truly to learn anything is also to learn about oneself: it is almost as if, like the ancient Egyptians, we place our hearts on the balance against the feather of Truth. But in the halls of Osiris, everything has already been done; now, and here, everything is yet to do.

One more analogy suggests itself in this connection: the intimate encounter that is eating and drinking. Do we merely look at what we study, or do we take it into ourselves? What we consume becomes a part of us; and we, by the same token, are changed by every mouthful. In *In the Vineyard of the Text*, his remarkable study of pre-scholastic attitudes to learning, Ivan Illich quotes Gregory the Great:

> Sacred scripture is sometimes food, sometimes drink for us. In the more obscure places, it is food, broken up through study, made nourishing through chewing. It is drink in the clearer places, and is absorbed as soon as it is read.[56]

Such concreteness may startle our fastidious cerebralism; but it reflects ways of thought whose roots go deep. The Latin *sapientia* derives from *sapere*, a verb which means 'to be wise, discerning, aware; to be in one's right mind'; but also, and originally, 'to taste'.

It is wisdom, as Kathleen Raine insisted, which 'should be the goal of all education': 'where the existing universities have increasingly failed, is to relate human studies to any unifying perspective of wisdom'.[57] The impoverished outlook which takes the goal of learning to be knowledgeability rather than wisdom has been with us for a long time. We see it in the Athenians of Saint Paul's day, who 'had no other recreation than saying or hearing the latest thing', and who responded with mockery when he called on them to 'feel' their way to God, and to repent (*metanoein*).[58]

Having related the parable of the sower, Jesus observed to his disciples that his hearers were themselves like the unproductive seeds of which he had spoken:

The heart of this people has been thickened, and they hear heavily with their ears, and they have closed their eyes – lest they should see with their eyes, and hear with their ears, and understand with their hearts, and turn again; and lest I should heal them.[59]

The opening of eyes and ears goes together with the opening of hearts, and with the transformation (*epistrophe*) of lives. What can follow from such transformation is described in the culmination of the parable:

The one sown upon the good earth, he is the one who hears and understands the word, and who bears fruit. One produces a hundred, another sixty, another thirty.[60]

Fruitfulness should be the aspiration of every teacher, and of every student.

VIII

*To make Temenos known to all those
who may benefit from its work*

'WHEN THE MYSTERIES ARE MADE PUBLIC, they are debased; and they lose their grace when they are profaned. Do not, therefore, cast pearls before swine, or strew roses for an ass to lie upon.' These words appear on the title page of *The Chemical Wedding of Christian Rosenkreutz*, published in 1616.[61] They present us with an obvious paradox: for this warning against publishing secret things introduces a published work. For all the recalcitrance of its veiled imagery, the *Wedding* is still a message addressed to the world; and yet what it tells us is that what it is telling us should not be told.

The same paradox is present in the teachings of Christ, whom the author of the *Wedding* quotes. On the one hand, he warns against casting pearls before swine, or giving that which is holy to dogs;[62] but on the other he enjoins his followers to go forth and teach 'all the peoples'.[63] The contrast is even more compactly present in the parable of the sower, already invoked in the editorial to *TAR* 14.[64] The image of seed being scattered beside the road, in stony places, or among thorns suggests an extravagant lack of discrimination, of which no actual sower would be guilty. Yet when the disciples ask Christ why he is speaking to the crowd in parables, he replies: 'Because it has been given to you to know the mysteries of the kingdom of heaven, but it has not been given to them.'[65]

These ambiguities can inform our reflections on the eighth of the Principles that inspire the work of the Temenos Academy, one which might otherwise seem straightforward enough as part of the brief of an educational charity: *To make Temenos known to all those who may benefit from its work.*

The universal dissemination of a message has never been easier. If the advent of radio and television seemed, in the twentieth century, to be bringing all humanity together, these media have now been subsumed and surpassed by the Internet and its associated technologies. More and more is it the case that almost everyone can communicate with almost everyone else; that almost everyone can, through a website or a blog, present himself or herself to the world. More and more of all that is being written, and of all that has been written, is within the reach of anyone with access to a laptop. We have come to take it for granted that dictionaries and maps and statistics, addresses and telephone numbers and timetables, should be instantly at our disposal; and we are indignant, and often helpless, if we encounter even a momentary obstruction to such availability.

Plainly, there are many ways in which the Temenos Academy could be broadcasting its name and work around the world; equally plainly, it has made only a modest use of these abundant opportunities. This is not due to timidity, or to lethargy, or to an unreasoning aversion to the new. Rather, it reflects awareness of a need for judicious caution in making use of information technology.

It is easy to heap up complaints about all of the rubbish and nonsense that are to be found on the Internet, or about all of the foolish and exploitative uses to which it can be put. These are matters of legitimate concern, but they are not the issue here. At the heart of the matter is a fundamental question of consciousness: for whatever purpose we may be using it, in what *state of mind* are we when we interact with a computer?

Every form of communication entails a distinct mode of awareness, and each of these modes harbours its own possibilities: recognition of this truth is reflected in the importance accorded, even in highly literate societies, to the memorization and recitation of the Vedic hymns, of the Qur'ān, or of the Homeric epics. When we speak or listen, the breath which carries the word, the conscious or unconscious empathy of speaker and hearer, all of the ineffable particulars of an encounter, invest the act of dialogue or declamation with far more than mere language can convey. When we write or read, we step out of the immediate world into a place where time moves differently, and where space no longer matters: we hear a silent voice, which may show us an invisible world. Both hearing and reading open up new spaces for us, in which there can be room to grow or to awake. Such virtual spaces constitute the *temenos*, the sacred enclosure which our Academy seeks to frame with its lectures, seminars and publications.

When we enter the sphere of the Internet we can enjoy the illusion of limitless space; but there is no stillness, and hence no place of sanctuary. I do not think that my own experience is atypical: when I sit at a keyboard my feeling is usually one of haste, of being on the move, of being tugged from one thing to the next. It can be an effort to read more than a page or two, and my relationship with information is predominantly *instrumental*: I am easily contented with the mere surfaces of facts, taking no more than I require to meet some immediate need. And then I am off again, a little giddy with all that is spread out before me, my brain already groping toward its next stimulus.

To say all this is not to condemn the Internet itself – a monument of human ingenuity, and a tool of extraordinary power and usefulness. What is problematical is our relationship with that tool, and here I think that two points should be made. The first is that, as I have already indicated, this technology conduces by its very nature to hurry, to distraction, to superficiality: it is opposed to that calming and deepening of thought which open the eyes of the spirit. Second: we must reckon with the Internet's *glamour*, in both the current and the older senses of that word. It has the power to charm us, to addict us, to enchant us; to persuade us that the buzzing tunnels of its labyrinth are where we find reality. Under such a spell we can become like those to whom Christ did not disclose the meaning of his parables: 'Seeing, they do not see; and hearing, they do not hear or understand'.[66]

The Latin counterpart of *temenos* is *fanum*: the 'pro-fane' is what lies outside the limits of the sacred enclosure. Although, as Keith Critchlow pointed out in the first issue of the original *Temenos*, 'strictly speaking there is no such thing as profane space', all the same 'profanation *can* exist'.[67] It exists, of course, in the spaces of the mind; here, as *The Chemical Wedding* warns us, the mysteries 'lose their grace when they are profaned'.

Let us return to the practical question of how Temenos is to be brought to the notice of those who are in search of what we strive to offer. Ultimately, I think that the answer is a simple one; but that simplicity should not lead us to ignore the profundity of the underlying issues.

We should make use of all legitimate means that come to hand in order to make ourselves known. In an age in which channels of communication seem constantly to be multiplying, we must not shy away from further possibilities merely because they are innovative and unfamiliar.

At the same time, we must not be seduced into communicating for communication's sake. We are guardians of a treasure beyond price; and we must always be vigilant lest that treasure be cheapened in the name of 'accessibility', lest compromises be made in the attempt to render our message more attractive or more 'relevant'. All are invited to enter the *temenos*; but it must not cease to be a sanctuary.

This means that care must be taken in considering not only what we teach, but how it is to be taught. We cannot sacrifice the conditions which make possible a reverent attention, a reflective understanding, the cherishing of the sacred. For all its effectiveness as a mechanism for distributing knowledge, the new technology does not seem to offer a space for the patience, the humility, the self-questioning, the penetration of layer after layer of meaning, which constitute the path toward the mysteries: to this end, the older vehicles of the word are still the best. Difficult though striking a balance always is, we must cultivate the art of scattering the seed without casting away the pearls.

indeed!

IX

*Reminding ourselves and those we teach
to look up and not down*

REMINDING OURSELVES AND THOSE WE TEACH *to look up and not down*. In endeavouring to expound the principles guiding Temenos, much of my task in previous editorials has been the fleshing out of abstract formulations: 'wisdom', 'vision', 'civilization', 'tradition' and the like. Here the situation is different. We are confronted with the concrete enigma of a symbolic utterance, which our habits of mind require us to recast in conceptual terms. What does it mean to 'look up'? What does it mean to 'look down'?

Setting out to compose a lecture on 'The Vertical Dimension', eventually included in the final issue of the journal *Temenos*, Kathleen Raine discovered that 'when I came to put pen to paper I found such a flood of thoughts pressing in on me that it seemed I could not even begin'.[68] I experience a similar difficulty now.

Where she did begin was with the image of the ladder in Jacob's vision: 'the top of it reached to heaven: and behold the angels of God ascending and descending upon it'.[69] While this clearly relates to our theme, it calls it into question also, for the angels go down as well as up. Heraclitus likewise laconically observed: '[The] road up, down: one and the same'.[70] The primary scripture of the alchemical tradition, the Emerald Tablet of Hermes Trismegistus, contains the even more radical assertion that 'what is below is like what is above, and what is above is like what is below, to accomplish the miracles of a single thing'.[71]

In fact, of course, there is not really a contradiction here. What is in question is not the spatial relationship between 'above' and 'below', but rather the quality of our attention – whither we should direct our gaze. For Plato, whose upward-pointing finger is his identifying attribute in Raphael's *School of Athens*, it is looking up which makes us human. He has Socrates say:

> The word 'man' (*anthrōpos*) signifies this: that the other animals neither observe nor examine nor consider nor look up (*anathrei*); but man has both observed – that is, he has seen (*opōpe*) – and he looks up, and he considers what he has seen. Hence, alone among the beasts, man was rightly called *anthrōpos*: 'looking up at what he has seen' (*anathrōn ha opōpe*).[72]

Animals, by contrast, lacking the upright posture of humanity, are beings 'neither making use of philosophy, nor looking (*athrountōn*) at all at the nature of heaven', with their heads 'drawn to the earth'.[73]

Many statements to the same effect can be found elsewhere in the writings of Plato, and in the Platonic tradition as a whole. Needless to say, Plato's 'up' is ultimately a metaphor, with only an analogical relationship to physical space. In Kathleen Raine's words, 'what is at issue is not any question of "another world" but the manner in which we experience this one. The vertical dimension is in the beholder.'[74] When the Psalmist says 'I will lift up mine eyes unto the hills, from whence cometh my help. My help cometh from the Lord, which made heaven and earth',[75] it is clear that he does not mean that God is in 'the hills' in any literal sense. Rather, the raising of our bodily eyes can shift our thoughts toward a Reality which transcends all directions. When Blake saw the world in a grain of sand, and Traherne perceived that 'the dust and stones of the street were as precious as gold',[76] they were looking *up* in this sense even as their faces were turned downward.

Finding in the 'vertical dimension', so understood, 'a hierarchy of states of consciousness which are themselves the agents which create different "worlds"', Kathleen Raine went on to assert that 'the vertical comparison is the key to the power of the symbol'.[77] The essential realities are above, while their contingent reflections lie here beneath. Or, in the words of Eriugena:

we should accept that by the name 'heaven' the principal causes of the intelligible and celestial essences have been signified; by the appellation 'earth', on the other hand, [the principal causes] of sensible things, with which the whole of this bodily world is filled.[78]

It is in these terms that the order by which all beings should be guided is to be found *above*. The symbolic language in which Christ taught his disciples to pray that his Father's will be done 'on earth as it is in heaven' finds its counterpart in China, where comprehension of *t'ien ming*, the 'will of heaven' which governs the rise and fall of earthly dynasties, was regarded by Confucius as one of the crucial realisations of his later maturity.[79] From heaven comes the pattern that is the source of the Tao.[80] In India, the liberated Self rises from the body to 'the highest flame' (*paraṁ jyotis*).[81]

And what of looking *down*? There are different ways of doing this. There is the view from the top of Jacob's ladder, the apprehension of all things *sub specie aeternitatis*. But there is also the downward gaze of those who believe that nothing above them exists – a reductive, scientistic analysis which understands all things in terms of lower, not of higher causes. This is an attitude made visible in the curved back of Blake's Newton, as he stoops over his diagrams oblivious of the mysteries of the larger world. It is a mode of seeing which affords great scope for cleverness, and for the worldly power which cleverness can serve; but none for wonder, or for wisdom.

In its final issue, Kathleen Raine described the original *Temenos* as 'a Review dedicated to affirming, defining, attempting to re-establish, that vertical dimension'.[82] In the same issue she announced the founding of the Temenos Academy, which has sought to remain faithful to this vision.

X

*Governance of the Temenos Academy itself
in light of the above Principles*

BEGINNING WITH *TAR* 9, the editorials in this journal have taken as their theme the ten Principles that inspire the work of Temenos. With this issue we reach the last in the series: *Governance of the Temenos Academy itself in light of the above Principles.*

As a teaching institution, Temenos operates through the word – in lectures, in seminars, in publications – and it exists to articulate and to advocate high ideals. So it is crucially important that we be on our guard lest what we do should be *only* words, and lest our service to those ideals be no more than lip service. It is appropriate to be reminded of this, after the inspiring litany of the other Principles. It is right that this should be included as one of the Principles, and right that it should come last. But that rightness is so evident that it leaves little else to say: to try to spin the subject out would lead to little that was not trite, or even sanctimonious.

In light of this, I shall take the liberty of writing about an aspect of the governance of the Academy which may seem to have little to do with the Principles, as they have been formally articulated. I believe however that it is at the very least compatible with them, and that it is probably ultimately inseparable from them as well.

The original journal *Temenos*, although it had four founders, was throughout nearly the whole of its existence edited by Kathleen Raine alone; and it was of course she who founded the Temenos Academy, and appointed its first Fellows and Academic Board. It is not merely that Temenos owes its existence to her; it owes its nature to her as well. In ways both describable and indescribable, it bears the imprint of her character: at its heart lies not a doctrinal system, but the richness of a human personality.

The practical consequences of this were dauntingly evident to the Academic Board when Kathleen Raine announced her intention to retire. Since its establishment, she had given the Academy its living unity: a unity which, like her own nature, was a dynamic array of contrasts. Kathleen Raine was both poet and scholar, both traditionalist and rebel, both contemplative and militant, a Londoner who only felt at home on the Scottish Borders – or in India. All of these elements cohered in her, and they have cohered in Temenos as well. But what would maintain that coherence when her presence was withdrawn? Each of us on the Board had been chosen as representing one or another aspect of what she cherished: could such an assemblage of individuals provide the same guiding spirit?

I remember our discussions at the time. We recognised that we could not fill the gap which Kathleen Raine was leaving; what we could collectively do, however, was to attempt still to represent the range and variety of her interests and values. Each of us, naturally, had distinct tastes and preferences and ideas of the True; and each of us would – and should – endeavour to pursue and further these. But we would not try to sway the Academy to our own ends, so that Temenos would become the vehicle of a single programme or agenda. Rather than going in one direction, or in another, Temenos should grow and thrive in the whole of itself. So far, thanks to the dedicated efforts of very many, I believe that it has done so; and to this extent we have been faithful to our trust.

What I am saying can easily give rise to at least two misunderstandings. It might seem that I am describing a personality cult, and an attempt to keep Temenos frozen in time as a monument to Kathleen Raine's memory. Any such effort would be futile and fundamentally wrong, as well as being a grievous betrayal of her own intentions. Like any healthy living creature, Temenos is constantly changing; and like any healthy child, it is not a mere replica of its parent. Paradoxically, one of the most precious things that the Temenos Academy owes to having had a single founder is the multitude of differences that it comprehends. In words of Blake which Kathleen Raine liked to quote:

'I never made friends but by spiritual gifts,/By severe contentions of friendship & the burning fire of thought'.[83]

It might also seem that in speaking of many perspectives, none of which should drown out the rest, I am advocating relativism – a refusal to recognise that any opinion is better than any other. Votaries of the Perennial Philosophy, whose concept of 'paths that lead to the same summit' is anything but relativist, will not be likely to take my words in such a spirit; but I think that something should be said to address this issue all the same. There is a profound difference between refraining from an insistence on the exclusive truth of a single vision, and holding all visions to be of equal value. At the apex of every mystical tradition is the acknowledgement of a Reality that lies so utterly beyond all human speech and thought as virtually to negate them: to say that our truest utterance must fall far short of the True is not to say that no words are truer than any others. Bearing witness to this Reality, and to the innumerable ways in which the inspired Imagination has sought it through all the ages of humanity, we celebrate the holy multiplicity which Kathleen Raine recognised. As she wrote:

> I have found
> A myriad particles
> And each is all
> That can ever be told,
> But all are inscribed
> With a signature
> That I cannot read.[84]

NOTES

1 *Chanson de Roland* lxxix (line 1015); *The Song of Roland: Text of the Oxford MS*, with an English translation by René Hague (London: Faber & Faber, 1937).

2 Qur'ān 5:48; cited from the translation by Marmaduke Pickthall, *The Glorious Koran* (New York: Alfred A. Knopf, 1930).

3 'A Vision of the Last Judgment'; *Blake: Complete Writings*, ed. Geoffrey Keynes, rev. ed. (Oxford: Oxford University Press, 1966), p. 617.

4 'The Presence'; *The Collected Poems of Kathleen Raine* (Ipswich: Golgonooza Press, 2000), p. 287.

5 'In Praise'; *Living with Mystery* (Ipswich: Golgonooza Press, 1992), p. 47.

6 Isaiah 6:3.

7 'A Song of Liberty'; Keynes, p. 160.

8 Psalm 82:6 (Authorised Version).

9 *Cherubinischer Wandersmann* II §83; *Johann Scheffler's (Angelus Silesius) sämmtliche poetische Werke*, ed. David August Rosenthal, 2 vols (Regensburg: Georg Joseph Manz, 1862), ii.38.

10 'What is Civilization?' first appeared in *Albert Schweitzer Jubilee Book*, ed. A. A. Roback (Cambridge MA: Sci-Art, 1946), pp. 261–74; it was reprinted by Brian Keeble in *What is Civilisation? and Other Essays* (Ipswich: Golgonooza Press, 1989), pp. 1–12.

11 *Inferno* VIII.69, XVIII.28–33, XXI.7–15.

12 *De ciuitate Dei* I, Preface.

13 *Scienza nuova*, edition of 1744, §1106; cited from *The New Science of Giambattista Vico*, trans. Thomas Goddard Bergin and Max Harold Fisch, revised and abridged ed. (New York: Doubleday Anchor, 1961), p. 381.

14 Psalm 122:3 (Authorised Version).

15 *Protagoras* 322c.

16 *Atharva Veda* 10.2.30.

17 *Orthodoxy* (London: John Lane, 1909), pp. 82–3.

18 Proverbs 8:22–32 (Authorised Version).

19 'A Vision of the Last Judgment'; Keynes, p. 611.

20 *Rig Veda* 1.105.12.
21 *Odyssey* XIX.108–14.
22 Job 28:26–7 (Authorised Version).
23 Proverbs 29:18 (Authorised Version).
24 'A Vision of the Last Judgment'; Keynes, p. 605.
25 Śāntideva, *The Bodhicaryāvatāra*, trans. Kate Crosby and Andrew Skilton (Oxford: Oxford University Press, 1998), p. 5.
26 'Tochmarc Étaíne', ed. Osborn Bergin and R. I. Best, *Ériu* 12 (1934–8) 137–96: p. 180.
27 *Immram Brain*, ed. Séamus Mac Mathúna (Tübingen: Max Niemeyer, 1985), p. 36 §19.
28 John 3:6–8 (Authorised Version).
29 Mark 7:8; cf. Matthew 15:6.
30 Galatians 1:13–14.
31 *Bhagavad Gītā* 11.42; trans. *Śrimad Bhagavad Geeta* (Delhi: Shree Geeta Ashram, 1978), p. 43.
32 *Christianity: Lineaments of a Sacred Tradition* (Edinburgh: T. & T. Clark, 1998), pp. 1–26: p. 11.
33 Ibid., p. 13.
34 Ibid., p. 22.
35 *TAR* 8 (2005) 64–77: pp. 74-5. This essay was first published in *Alexandria* 1 (1991) 19–35.
36 Ibid., p. 72.
37 Ibid., p. 73.
38 Philip Sherrard's posthumously published essay 'Kathleen Raine and the Symbolic Art', *TAR* 11 (2008) 180–208, elicited Jack Herbert's 'Philip Sherrard on "Kathleen Raine and the Symbolic Art": Some Reactions and Thoughts', *TAR* 12 (2009) 238–47.
39 *Yannehāsti na tat kvacit*: *Mahābhārata* 1.56.33; cf. *The Mahābhārata: 1. The Book of the Beginning*, trans. J. A. B. van Buitenen (Chicago: University of Chicago, 1973), p. 130. The same phrase is cited from the *Viśvasāra Tantra* by Arthur Avalon (Sir John Woodroffe), *The Serpent Power*, 2nd rev. ed. (Madras: Ganesh, 1924), p. 50 and n. 2.
40 *Dhammapada* §276; cited from T*he Dhammapada*, trans. Juan Mascaró (Harmondsworth: Penguin, 1973).
41 Cited in *Lighting a Candle: Kathleen Raine and Temenos* (London: Temenos Academy, 2008), p. 19.
42 'Revisioning the Sacred', p. 68.
43 'Editorial: The Arts and the Imagination', *Temenos* 1 (1981) 1–6: p. 5.
44 Quoted from the *Nafaḥāt al-uns* by Annemarie Schimmel, *Mystische Dimensionen des Islam: Die Geschichte des Sufismus* (Frankfurt am Main: Insel, 1995), p. 314.
45 *Pensées* §646.

46 Text ed. Édouard Jeauneau, *'Lectio philosophorum': Recherches sur l'École de Chartres* (Amsterdam: Adolf M. Hakkert, 1973), p. 38.

47 Mary Brennan, 'Materials for the Biography of Johannes Scottus Eriugena', *Studi medievali* 3rd series, 27:1 (1986) 413–60: p. 431.

48 *Discours sur la méthode* IV.

49 *Temenos* 6 (1985) 5–11: p. 10.

50 *Islamic Art and Spirituality* (Ipswich: Golgonooza Press, 1987), pp 17–36: p. 21.

51 *Art and a Changing Civilisation* (London: John Lane, 1934), pp. 135–6.

52 *The Dance of Śiva: Fourteen Indian Essays* (New York: The Sunwise Turn, 1918), p. 127.

53 *Temenos Academy Inaugural Addresses* (London: Temenos Academy, 1992), pp. 13–21: pp. 17–18. This address has been republished in *Lighting a Candle*, pp. 157–65.

54 *Seventh Letter* 344b–c.

55 *Dhammapada* §§19, 64; trans. Mascaró, pp. 37, 44.

56 *Moralia in Iob* I.29; cited by Ivan Illich, *In the Vineyard of the Text: A Commentary to Hugh's Didascalicon* (Chicago: University of Chicago, 1993), p. 55.

57 *Lighting a Candle*, p. 97.

58 Acts 17:21, 27, 30–32.

59 Matthew 13:15.

60 Matthew 13:23.

61 Reproduced as the frontispiece to *The Chemical Wedding of Christian Rosenkreutz*, trans. Joscelyn Godwin (Grand Rapids: Phanes Press, 1991).

62 Matthew 7:6; cf. 15:26.

63 Matthew 28:19.

64 Matthew 13:3–23, Mark 4:2–20, Luke 8:4–15.

65 Matthew 13:11.

66 Matthew 13:13.

67 'TEMENOS or Temples, Cosmic Rhythms and the Universality of Sacred Space', *Temenos* 1 (1981) 211–19: p. 211.

68 *Temenos* 13 (1992) 195–212: p. 195.

69 Genesis 28:12 (Authorised Version).

70 Diels-Kranz, fragment 60.

71 Cited in Julius Ruska, *Tabula Smaragdina: Ein Beitrag zur Geschichte der hermetischen Literatur* (Heidelberg: Carl Winter, 1926), p. 2.

72 *Cratylus* 399c.

73 *Timaeus* 91e.

74 'The Vertical Dimension', p. 198.

75 Psalm 121:1–2 (Authorised Version).

76 *Centuries* iii.3.

77 'The Vertical Dimension', p. 204.

78 *Periphyseon* ii.546b; *Iohannis Scotti Eriugenae Periphyseon (De Diuisione*

Naturae) liber secundus, ed. I. P. Sheldon-Williams (Dublin: Dublin Institute for Advanced Studies, 1983), pp. 48–50.

79 *Analects* ii.4.
80 *Doctrine of the Mean* §1.
81 *Chandogya Upaniṣad* 8.3.4.
82 'The Vertical Dimension', p. 195.
83 'Jerusalem', chapter 4; Keynes, p. 738.
84 'On a Shell-strewn Beach'; *Collected Poems*, p. 330.